Whitethorn

Whitethorn

POEMS

JACQUELINE OSHEROW

LOUISIANA STATE UNIVERSITY PRESS
BATON ROUGE

Published with the assistance of the Sea Cliff Fund

Published by Louisiana State University Press
Copyright © 2011 by Jacqueline Osherow
All rights reserved
Manufactured in the United States of America
LSU Press Paperback Original
First printing

Designer: Laura Roubique Gleason
Typeface: Minion Pro
Printer and binder: IBT Global, Inc.

Poems in this volume appeared previously in the following publications:
*American Poetry Review, Antioch Review, Barrow Street, Colorado Review,
The Forward, Jewish Quarterly, Michigan Quarterly Review, New Ohio Review,
New Republic, Northwest Review, Pleiades, Ploughshares, Poetry Daily, Prairie
Schooner, Southwest Review,* and *Yale Review.*

The author is grateful to the Eastern Frontier Educational Foundation,
Hedgebrook, PEN Flanders, the Utah Arts Council, and the University of Utah
Research Committee for their support and to Wayne Koestenbaum and Barry
Weller for their invaluable help with this book.

LIBRARY OF CONGRESS CATALOGING-IN-PUBLICATION DATA
Osherow, Jacqueline.
  Whitethorn : poems / Jacqueline Osherow.
    p. cm.
  ISBN 978-0-8071-3835-9 (pbk. : alk. paper)
  I. Title.
  PS3565.S545W55 2011
  811'.54—dc22

                          2010038290

For Anne Brodke, Deborah Feder, Aaron Fogelson, Lisa Keida, Beth Levine, and Mazal Peterson, who drove my children so I could write this book

and, of course, for Jenne Parsons

Contents

I

Poem for Jenne

Larkspur and delphinium, wild and tame
transcriptions of the same essential idiom
(as lullaby, corralled, is requiem,
a sigh, bound and gagged, a lyric poem).

Earth's trying to remake herself with stars,
her own inky domain of skyey colors.
She wants everything. It won't be hers.

Her starry flowers, heedless of safeguards,
will launch their blue and purple rockets heavenwards
and leave her to her dusty browns and reds,
her brief sky shattered, just as words—

the good ones, anyway—will quit this page
before I ever pay this garden homage
or name the pain I'm trying to assuage.

Nonetheless, these clusters *are* in flower
if only for an instant, as they were
a year ago, when Jenne (this poem's for her),
knowing how I love them, put them here

to make the way around my house less bitter.
My next-door neighbor, she'd watched things shatter
and so came by to plant and tend and water

and whatever else it is that gardeners do.
And I remember catching a dim glimpse, as if through
an impossible tunnel—*what's all that blue?*—
and thinking, as one thinks of something wholly out of view,

how lovely it would be to lay my eyes on them,
though they were there, waiting, each time I came home:
larkspur out the back, out front delphinium

(the cultivated version for the public eye,
its wild incarnation just for me . . .)
and once or twice I did suspect that beauty
and kindliness had aimed themselves my way

but each was such a difficult abstraction,
at best unverifiable, uncertain,
a meteor I wasn't sure I'd seen.

I, who'd been so lucky up to then,
was utterly astonished by what pain—
in its purest form—can make out of a person.
It was (such things exist) a brutal season

and one that's not entirely departed
though time has passed; flowers, twice, have sprouted.
The earth will be, twice over, broken-hearted,

which means, at least according to King David,
in his most unnerving psalm, closer to God.
Me? I'd leave some distance if I could
though it would be untrue to say no good

has come from any of this. See? out my window
the earth again has sheathed herself in indigo;
this may be the time she makes it through:

her sapphire daggers, bursting their scabbards,
carve frantic constellations: elfin songbirds
vehement with blue and purple chords;
earth's reaching for her heavens, I for words

or any chink of rapture I can claim.
Delphinium. Larkspur. Larkspur. Delphinium.
Let me claim you as you climb and climb.

Proust on the Slow Train from Grosseto

I missed the last bus and had to take the train,
an absurd route (I traced it on a map)
like New York to Philly, via Boston—

checking in at every little station stop
in western Tuscany, the order random.
But I had open treasure on my lap:

what Italians call *Le Ricerche,* the first volume
(a plural, since no singular sufficed,
the multiple *Researches of Lost Time*).

In truth, the antique carriage suited Proust,
its start-and-stop, its slow eccentric rhythm,
each square of sky intensely overcast

and then split open by a full-fledged storm
so that I kept moving from the young Marcel's
interwoven overlays of daydream

to lightning startling olive-dotted hills,
which echoed with the opera that each station
improvised from greetings and farewells.

I'd lose some crucial thread or convolution
as another chance quartet reached its crescendo
and have to keep rereading the same section

looking for the hidden innuendo
of whatever unassuming word or phrase
had been darkened by a raindrop through my window.

I was reading PLACE-NAMES: THE PLACE—
in which the potent, not yet sounded syllables
of names of towns were unrepeated mantras

that, once uttered, cast enduring spells.
I knew the actual cities but forgot them—
preferred the more ethereal towers and hills

of words' exquisite forays into dream,
not that Proust in any way fails Venice
(the one Italian city he could claim

as a nodding acquaintance, face-to-face
from his terrace on the Riva degli Schiavoni),
but his way of capturing the unseen grace

of a place just from its name was so uncanny
that I looked out my window in disbelief
at that fake landscape posturing as Tuscany,

the real one on my haunches, keeping safe.
The storm that had propelled my little train
through all that falseness finally spent itself,

and without the constant urging of the rain
its languid pace grew even more lethargic;
the sky went dark in earnest; night came on,

my window's black so thick it seemed opaque
and there I was, at last, uninterrupted,
reading like some emptied-out amnesiac,

so lost in the dominion I'd adopted
I mistook it for my own imagining,
everything I'd known or seen co-opted

by what Proust's elliptic sorcery could wring
from the timbre of a city's withheld name.
There was nothing in that country as compelling

as his progress through the semi-dark delirium
in which I—if it was I—sat transfixed.
I'd have stayed forever in that steady hum

of thick, unhurried motion: train and text
driven by a not-yet-mentioned name.
No one will believe what happened next:

how the train, slower still, approached a platform
with its long, late, out-of-breath cortege,
how the letters on the sign chose exactly to conform

to what was just unfolding on my page:
as if the only word worth spelling were "Siena"
and geography were always paying homage

to the sway of syllables, unless Siena
really was a figment of Proust's dream.
Where was I? Would *that* Siena—

had I thought to disembark in time—
even have resembled the red mirage
perched around a black-and-white striped dome

where a high probing tower appears to rummage
through the heavens for the single hold-out angel
Duccio never managed to dislodge?

(The others, of course, had transferred, at his call,
to the gold arrested air around his Mary,
an environ far more splendid and ethereal

than the one they came from, and less illusory.
You couldn't call it anything but *Maestà*.)
It was probably Duccio's vision, albeit blurry,

puny, black-and-white—an early replica—
that launched the kyrie in Proust's ear
for that perfect one-word masterpiece: Siena,

an enchantment I not only got to hear
but to enter for an instant when my unhinged train
found its way to that precarious stratosphere

where a word will take on actual dimension
and those archrivals, clarity and mystery,
reveal themselves, at heart, to work in unison.

I was so hell-bent on chasing beauty
it almost seems, in retrospect, inevitable,
my stumbling on that out-of-balance trinity:

Siena, Proust, the endlessly insatiable—
if utterly uncomprehending—me,
wrong about everything conceivable.

How could I have failed to see the misery
weighing down each gold-encrusted angel?
that Proust had fabricated his soliloquy

as an urgent plea for somewhere to install
his treasury of unrequited emotion?
The usual repositories were full:

each heart on earth oblivious or taken,
crude or limited or cracked or fallible
or permanently broken, like his own.

No doubt it was supremely beautiful
but I missed its one essential lesson.
Frankly, I didn't have the wherewithal

(I'd yet to have my own disastrous run-in
with that conscientious hitman, life on earth),
the inner points of reference to take in

what each deferred subjunctive clause was worth
in terms of irremediable sorrow.
I was spellbound more than moved. I held my breath

for three straight volumes. Twenty years ago.
All I knew of sadness was that restless
impatience with what youth defines as narrow,

in my case: the semi-detached house
where I first knew Siena as a reddish-brown
crayon color—one I rarely chose—

darker than the brick tone of the earthbound town
that gave asylum to those stateless angels
undone by all their years of looking down.

What made me so certain that their troubles
had nothing whatsoever to do with me?
were merely alien Christian details

from which I could extract my graven quantity
of undiluted beauty and move on?
To think that I looked on with them at Mary—

inconsolable—holding her infant son
without even the slightest hint of warning
that this is what it is to mother children.

Why was I incapable of learning
anything I didn't already know?
I thought I was watching my own yearning,

could almost feel the heft of my own halo
invisible as theirs were, gold on gold.
I was a kid then, reader. Twenty years ago.

I have been young, but now am old.
Too old, I'm afraid, to tell the story
I meant to tell here. It can't be told

(the one about the language so incantatory
I watched it conjure up an actual town)
without at least acknowledging that Mary

presides over it all awash in pain.
Why have my troubles come as a surprise?
Haven't I stared at crucifixion after crucifixion

where Mary tries and fails to shield her eyes?
She can't do a thing for her child either
and she, by all accounts, is selfless, wise,

giving, gentle, kind, the ideal mother.
What hope has there ever been for me?
I tried to redress this with a father.

How was I to know that he'd go crazy?
But let's not dwell on that. What's lost is lost.
The point is, now it's wholly up to me

and I'm here writing about Siena and Proust,
my failure, years ago, to heed their warning,
when I have a daughter who is too hard-pressed

to leave her bed on any given morning.
Here's the difference between life and art:
there's no gold here, or incense burning,

no grace in the mother who gives no comfort,
but stands around, useless, looking on.
So do me a favor, reader, avert

your eyes. Focus on Mary and her son,
how beautiful they are; leave me out of this;
what I have to teach, no one can learn.

You'd have to have spent your life oblivious,
distracted by that fugitive domain
to which gold leaf and tempera bear witness

as the perfume of a tea-soaked madeleine
offers details of a vanished trove of marvels
glimpsed in passing from a wayward train

unfettered by departures or arrivals.
Don't ask me how I've lived for all these years
without suspecting that life unravels.

Don't ask me anything. I left my answers
in the carriage of a discontinued train,
on the left-hand window seat, inside the covers

of a book I've always meant to read again
to find out if its death-defying prose
shares the virtue of its hero's madeleine,

if, rereading, I'd be back inside my gatehouse
above a doll-sized Florence, on a ridge
whose likenesses in half a dozen frescoes

frame the magi's bulky entourage,
if the vineyards, cypresses, and olive groves
would yield again to each unfolding passage

refined by the resistant coos of doves.
Who knows? Perhaps I'd relocate a cluster
of half-scrawled papers stashed behind some shelves,

some hieroglyphic fissures in the plaster
chiseled by the scraping of my jangling foot
as those half-redeemed epiphanies came faster.

All I want is one undamaged thought,
one clear, identifiable reminder
that life is not entirely defeat,

some remnant of that shameless sense of wonder
that led me so wholeheartedly astray.
I need to come up with a rejoinder

to what my daughter doesn't bother to say,
an offering so irresistible
that she'll want to wrest from each new day

its allocation of the inexhaustible,
the very thing that sent me off to Italy,
to daydream, my Proust face down on the table.

You see, reader, it *does* come back to me:
the sputtering lamp (a short), the lumpy chair,
the castle out my window (thirteenth-century)

eclipsed by what the flickering of my fire
(my only source of heat) could help me conjure:
mostly, I was fashioning a future

so full it crowded out the wanting air.
At the center of my charmed Italian sojourn
was a heart that had too much room to spare.

I'd dream up things to long for, watch them burn,
more riveting than frescoes and cathedrals.
Amazing what necessity will make you learn:

mornings, I'd dig out the burning coals
I'd covered up with ash the night before,
touch them to a pair of homemade spills

(even now, I could revive a day-old fire)
and watch my breath immediately scatter
into blue and orange outposts of desire:

everything I longed for joined the clutter
self-combusting, and at its core
(is this all I have to give my daughter

from so much time among that Tuscan treasure?
dreams and their circuitous trajectory?)
are my burning imaginings of her . . .

not even remotely satisfactory
compared to her real-life incarnation.
Real life does sometimes manage a victory

over even the greediest imagination.
Nothing prepared me for my children:
my perfect instant at the Siena station,

only perpetual, the words *and* place my own . . .
and this time, there were people on the platform,
exquisitely familiar, but unknown,

their claim on me so urgent and extreme
that, for once in my life, I longed for nothing,
pitied dreamers the paucity of dream,

still pity them, in spite of everything;
I even pity that young girl on the train
so entranced, she barely knows she's breathing—

staring at the same page yet again,
then out the window, then off in space,
as if the spheres might let her listen in.

What if she'd stayed like that, poised to miss
her modicum of everything that matters?
She could not have borne such weightlessness.

So why can't I stop wishing that my daughters
might have had a fleeting chance to move
through that same landscape, without parameters,

no pain to speak of, no terror, no love,
no naming of their final destination,
their reveries as supple and elusive

as the route of their condemned, last-minute train,
its wheels, their musings, perfectly in tandem,
the windows blurred by sudden streaks of rain

until no passing sights are what they seem,
the universe an urgent invitation,
an incontrovertible barrage of dream.

Reading *The Makioka Sisters* on the Sidney / Anacortes Ferry

Tanizaki, San Juan Islands, biting wind.
I am dreaming a long unhurried ferry ride,
shy Yukiko still not yet a bride
as, one by one, each shapely gray-green island
reveals itself and slowly falls away.
Mount Baker vanishes, then comes again
just in time to stand in for Mount Fuji
as Sachiko spies it from a moving train.
People come out once in a while. "Good book?"
They take some pictures; one ex-marine
(unaware a firefly hunt has just begun)
even tries to hold a conversation.
But, happily, the wind makes it cold on deck.
Except for the Makiokas, they all go in.

Camouflage
(Useless Bay, Whidbey Island)

How untangle one gray from the other
when they're all one color: sea, heron, sky?
An odd color: changeable *and* steady,
the sort of thing a pearl's elderly mother
might put on once her husband passed away,
but, still, for widows' weeds, luminescent.
I've seen a moon this shade—tentative, crescent,
a shifting maze of storm clouds in its way—
manage, nonetheless, to rear its head
just as this heron does, despite the cloud
precisely the same color, right behind him.
He feels it too, doesn't he, both storm and calm?
A flash of lightning, thunder, disarray,
then that gray union: sea, sky, heron, me.

Autumn Cottonwood

These days there's not a thing I don't regret
but thanks anyway, emphatic cottonwood,
Ms. over-the-top gold backlit by storm cloud,
for trying to persuade me to get over it,
that each defective day is worth resuming.
Poor tree. You don't know what's coming.
Enjoy it while it lasts; I won't tell.
You'll find out soon enough. Fall is fall.
Unless you get used to losing everything?
Still, I wouldn't want to take your place.
My misfortune's relatively mild;
I've got piles of stuff; I'm even singing.
It was pure hubris—or was it avarice?—
to think I could hang on to all that gold.

Autobiographical: Another Draft

It looked like a fifties-movie version
of a mutant life form on a distant planet—
but I adored it with a needy passion,

called it my botanical Halley's Comet
since it would only bloom one day a year
or so the owner claimed when I sublet.

I'd prayed the bloom would come while I was there.
I'd work in New York—double shifts four days—
and then, for the next ten, would disappear

to write myself out of my malaise.
(Then, I'd have told you a long narrative,
but really it was just a basic case

of more or less unrequited love.)
My friends thought I was crazy, just to go
where I knew no one, to try to live;

I'd seen it in the *Voice:* sublet in Brattleboro—
two hundred dollars a month, walk to train . . .
a hillside and a river out the window.

I'd probably make the same choice again.
In any case, the blossom didn't come
which to me seemed perfectly in tune

with my own inanimate momentum.
Every passing minute was out of whack;
where would a flower find the space to bloom?

Don't misunderstand me. I wasn't sick;
I tried to write, would distract myself with a novel
(Willa Cather, I remember, *The Song of the Lark*)

but I lived for the mail's pointless arrival,
not that I didn't know the thing was hopeless
but I just couldn't make my hope unravel

or move myself to want anything else.
I'd drag myself to the library for more Cather:
O Pioneers! My Ántonia, The Professor's House,

one novel and then another and then another.
I think, once, I read three in one day—
nothing worked out for those people either—

and for quite a while I just went on that way:
proofreading graveyard every two weeks
after copyediting (a biweekly) during the day.

I tried out bits of poems, read more books;
The Raj Quartet (I'd finished all of Cather),
checked eight, nine times a morning in my mailbox

and then one evening it was simply there,
had been there, probably, all day,
so subtle and pervasive I was unaware

of its idiosyncratic company.
I half-thought it rose up off the page
from the hills of India—at least as likely

as my having just missed the entourage
of a furtive giantess, whose parting gift—
a gargantuan, over-the-top corsage—

had lured its whitish purples off a snowdrift
just before (or was it after?) sun had set.
I was beside myself, utterly bereft

when, racing to the back room, I caught sight of it
(by then, the scent had literally exploded
and I finally understood the bloom was out)

my squandered blossom . . . I'd been defrauded . . .
surely there were warning signs I'd missed . . .
why had I left it so long unattended?

Those sweet tentative phases gone unwitnessed.
When had the bud shed its green disguise?
More than half its day probably passed.

For as long as I could I wouldn't blink my eyes
but then it seemed absurd just to stand there.
What could I do but go about my business?

I went and brought my book, my reading chair
and sat down reading, I and the blossom
a mismatched but companionable pair,

my breath a medium for its perfume.
Maybe—I'm not sure—I even took a look
at an on-again, off-again poem;

I put one from those days in my first book.
We could say I began it that same night
but that would obscure the flower's more basic magic.

It wasn't what I did or didn't write
but rather that, albeit trumped-up or random,
I did have business to go about

or maybe that I, too, didn't have much time,
my one day a year was partly over.
I also ought to wear it as a diadem,

to cut myself away from what could never
right itself or make a start;
I took on faith what I would soon discover:

that it's a spacious place, a person's heart
and with that, gold was instantaneous:
a single branch at first, brazen, a flirt,

leaving telltale jewelry in the grass,
then deeper golds, gold-oranges, orange-reds
until it seemed as if some senile cosmos

had purged itself of all its perseids—
hillsides of vermilion fallen stars.
I saw them all as my blossom's hybrids

and their obliging gold stayed on for years.
I don't think I was sad for an entire decade.
Who had time? I had three daughters.

Besides, I was working on a method
to say just what I meant and make it rhyme.
I knew for a fact that life is good,

and started a celebratory poem
that would make this knowledge wholly clear—
but it turns out that, beneath it, all this time

(I've written drafts and drafts, year after year)
each line was bracing (what *did* I know
and who, I'm wondering, did I think would hear?)

to ask the question: where's that flower now?
When will it bloom again and get me out of this?
All this time, I was racing toward a sorrow

(it turns out, there are troubles worse than numbness,
than escaping to novels in a quiet room)
that would prove entirely impervious

to even the most vehement perfume.
Please don't, reader, press me for details.
Let's just say I've lost my equilibrium,

and am trying to maneuver through the shambles
to find solace for my three bewildered girls.
Those sad Vermont months spent reading novels

now seem to me like vanished pastorals.
There's bitterness in learning how to live
and my elaborate series of deferrals

has proved itself supremely ineffective.
I could make excuses; I *have* lost my way,
but there's no fixed route when you're a fugitive;

besides, I've got three girls. I have to stay
at least within striking distance of where I am,
wherever exactly that is. Things give way

and we're left to a long, uncertain interim.
Still, it wouldn't be accurate to say
I've been unlucky. I've had lots of time.
Some things blossom only for a day.

Sonnets from *The Song of Songs*

I (THORNS/FOREST)

I tried to write you a sonnet; it wouldn't work.
Here's what I would write if you weren't crazy
was the way it started. But you *are* crazy
so I just let the laptop screen go dark.
I wouldn't be writing if you weren't crazy;
you'd be here in the house somewhere, just back
from the morning's carpools, not that we'd talk:
you'd be off again on errands; I'd be busy
writing poems that now seem ill-conceived—
not one of them a love poem. Too late.
You could read *The Song of Songs*. I felt like that,
which explains how I lived the way I lived.
I was fearless once; I chose the rarest
apple tree among the trees of the forest.

II (BUDS/TURTLEDOVE)

This has to be the diametric opposite
of the buds' appearance, the song's arrival
but, shoveling snow, I almost pity Shulamit
who'll never know the earth as this insatiable,
this self-negating, this far gone, this white.
Gazelles or no gazelles, love does unravel.
She may want to lose herself in blankness.
Even my heart has left her hiding place
to try the famous palliative of ice,
our street's telltale details safely annulled:
I'd stay out with her all night—I love the cold—
until we're both completely covered over
(good luck to Shulamit with that young lover)
but I have kids to put to sleep, laundry to fold.

III (KISSES/WINE)

Let him kiss me with the kisses of his
mouth; let him kiss me with anything;
let him kiss me, let him remember once,
momentarily, that, once, he'd *kiss me* . . .
for your love is better. . . . Don't be absurd;
wine can never withstand much bitterness.
It was sung by a single voice, your song
of songs: yours, coming from your upstairs bed,
drowned out by his computer, his TV.
Don't you remember? This went on for years . . .
and you—I—was so (*let him kiss me*) dense,
I kept believing he'd come up the stairs.
Still, there are girls here. Our daughters. Three.
Surely (*with the kisses of his mouth*) he must have kissed me.

Snow in Umbria

Call it fate. Call it nature. Call it luck.
Call it unrepeatable euphoria.
Once in a hundred years, there's a freak
snowfall in the olive groves of Umbria

and I, by dint of miracle, was there.
(The windfall that had paid my charter fare:
an actual publication.) Even the moon
colluded in my spell of perfect fortune—

full that night, or one night shy of full,
deploying all its silver on the overthrow
of silver olive leaves by silver snow
to capture in their triple silver thrall

the footloose ghosts marooned at Trasimeno.
And I was scheduled to leave the very next day—
on a nonrefundable ticket—from Ciompino,
which meant that I would have to make my way

(after hitching six kilometers to the station—
unplowed—a brave trucker took me on)
through that elaborate blankness into Rome,
undaunted by its profligate amalgam

of incompatibility and union,
the mild vistas I had learned by heart
trammeled by this mesmerizing upstart,
my mute but intimate companion

on that static one-way crawl to Rome,
each stalled motion of my leaden train
another used-up portion of my lifetime's
unexpected share in that terrain,

so shot through with sun, once it came up
(I hitched and caught the local in pitch darkness,
dawn broke as I changed for the express)
I yielded to its dazzle the entire trip,

half-convinced that it was inexhaustible
and half that it was pure hallucination,
in no way ready for the rush of dull,
weirdly snowless trees against my train

somewhere near the balmy edge of Rome.
To think, spring after spring, how I'd done double-takes
at the sight of olives sneaking into bloom,
their puny, whitish blossoms so like snowflakes

I'd wonder how I'd failed to see them fall.
But snow in Umbria is unmistakable—
a thorough, if unabiding, revelation.
And I gave it up for the Rome station,

the anxious taxi ride, the crowded plane
boarded just in time, the shuttle, the A-train,
Amtrak, my father's retirement, my friend's wedding—
where I told again and again the tale of skidding,

clutching the couple's gift (fragile, ceramic)
in the spinning cab of an Italian truck
on a century's supply of Umbrian snow.
As for what I'd seen out my window,

I did try to describe it, but without success,
having left it irretrievably behind.
And then—what can I tell you?—so much happened
so quickly that I could barely focus

on any other thing—the usual reason.
I don't think I'll tell the story here
but 1985 was a banner year
for things that would never happen again

and Italy did resurface: the place to go
for our honeymoon. (Yes, reader. It came to that.
I, too, uncharacteristically, wore white;
once in a hundred years, a dress of snow.)

I was dumbstruck as we made our way from Rome;
the entire landscape so completely blighted,
I would have thought the train had been rerouted,
except that station names remained the same.

It was like a tour through Pharaoh's dream
with olive trees replacing cows and corn.
That's when I remembered Nonna's grim
pronouncement that the snow I loved would burn

her olive groves—so easy to ignore
as a piece of *contadina* superstition,
like the *messa nera,* her stock suggestion
when madness struck the village (a proven cure).

But those tracts and tracts of black diminished trees
bore all the hallmarks of a fire's path.
Is that where Petrarch got *I burn and freeze?*
He'd witnessed such a snow or, rather, its aftermath?

Ardendo il verno. In winter I burn.
They looked like sudden widows gathered to mourn
the freak disaster—shipwreck? mine explosion?—
that had swept away, in one quick blast, their men.

Umbria produced no oil for years
and its legacy of time-honored procedures
had nothing for what happens once a century.
Every grower had a different theory:

some cut back their trees; some cut them down;
a few dreamers left them as they were
and others did the same thing in despair.
Planting olives requires determination

since new trees won't give fruit for many years.
At Nonna's they tried a little of everything
and when I came next—1990, spring,
pregnant with the second of my daughters—

her olive groves looked like themselves again
except for the occasional black reminder,
which, up close, revealed a single, slender
but still incontrovertible shoot of green.

That live, green glimpse is why I'm here.
Though it's worth remarking: the selfsame year,
the selfsame requiem: once in a lifetime
and I *have* always meant to make a poem

of that short-lived union, olive and snow.
But just now, what I really need to know
or remember, rather, is not the dazzle
but the irrepressible, if slow, reprisal

of earth's unerring appetite for green—
not that it would really apply to me
or my children. Our catastrophe
(my own grove, it turns out, was not immune

to a like infestation of total blackness)
has nothing to do with olive cultivation.
I've been chasing after the wrong superstition.
Clearly what's required is the black mass,

not a rhapsody on olive groves in snow.
It is, in fact, a case of mental illness
(My ex-husband's. So now you know.)
though it wasn't my intention to go into this.

Impossible conjunctions were my subjects:
their purity, their brevity, their brilliance,
but I failed to factor in the zeal of retrospect's
unsparing imposition of surveillance

over what a clear-eyed person might have known—
should have known—the glints of warning,
by which I do not mean a landscape mourning
for the whole duration of a honeymoon;

that could—though it was not—have been coincidence,
but textbook symptoms, less and less obscure.
I always falter in the face of evidence,
hence my predilection for metaphor,

which is fairly difficult to carry off
once known parameters have come apart.
You lose all bearings; your mind's not safe
and that arbiter of last resort, your heart,

consigns itself to the ready paralysis
that doubles as a palliative for shock.
That green shoot growing out of black
was meant to instigate a metamorphosis.

It was wishful thinking, not metaphor.
I'm an eyewitness. Things endure
in the least accommodating situations.
You have to learn to shrink your expectations.

Unless you can't shrink them. Unless they burn.
I used to believe that I could learn
whatever it was I truly had to know.
But it's a humbling prospect, absorbing sorrow,

which no amount of learning will amend
and I'm not very graceful when I fail.
Meanwhile, there's no change in my ex-husband.
He's on the streets when he's not in jail.

Ci vuole la messa nera, as Nonna would say,
and, believe me, I'd give anything a try,
though, when she first said it, I was horrified,
that is, once I finally understood

the implications of her *sotto voce*
mutterings, half exposé, half reticence,
my friend, her grandson, mortified that I
should overhear such backward peasant nonsense.

Exorcism. In the late twentieth century.
But I'd adored every other peasant story:
cheating the nobles . . . drinking milk from a goat's teat . . .
though I *was* shaken when I'd left a note

only to find out she couldn't read.
So that was why she so cherished TV,
talked back to it, consoled it, always argued
with the deadpan anchorpeople on the *telegiornale,*

most vocal at the planned release from jail
of the Nazi who'd blown up a cathedral
with a thousand people crammed inside.
She took one look at the sick, old man and said

Let Jesus have mercy on him. I won't.
My view, precisely, with the Waffen-SS,
except for the part that has to do with Jesus.
Still, within a month, the man was sent

(despite his victims' families) back home
where he received a traditional hero's welcome
from the Austrian minister of defense.
It's an elusive business, recompense,

at best, flimsy or hypothetical,
at worst, as in the Nazi's case, obscene.
But even when it might be genuine,
its workings are as cryptic and elliptical

as the orbit of an undetected comet
primed for wreaking havoc on our stars.
Still, on balance, it's less approximate
than a number of our pet human endeavors,

each with its abstract, moving target.
Which is why I wish I'd paid attention,
at least heard Nonna out, asked a question
(it's always certainty that we regret)

when the *messa nera* surfaced as an option.
Not that it could ever provide a cure.
But cure had little part of its inception;
It's the rest of us the *messa nera*'s for:

onlookers, failed intimates of sickness,
half-thinking what we've loved might reappear.
We need some protocol to make us stare
directly in the face of total darkness

which is—how else to know this?—all that's there.
And I'm trying, reader. I really am.
But this may be the closest I can come
before some piece of loose, remembered silver

mounts its luminous counterattack:
even in memory, instantly over,
all-out devastation in its wake,
but still, reader, silver on silver

which no resulting blackness will take back.
Think what tricks the single-minded air
pulled off behind that skinflint nature's back
to lure away such hefty stores of silver:

five decades' gibbous moons bereft of aura,
lakes and rivers fleeced of half their glow.
Not even the perpetual *messa nera*
the trees held daily for three years or so

could make the unregenerate hills repent;
they'd felt what they'd felt, seen what they'd seen.
And surely some recovery was imminent;
there were rumors of the slow ascent of green.

Tulip Ode

Tulips! You're real heroes! You've come back!
I always knew you were the souls of kindness
and never fell for those ridiculous
rumors about your rising up like clockwork
every springtime from some ugly bulb.
As if such bounty could be perennial.
I like to call a miracle a miracle.
God—if He exists—is rarely glib.
Besides—am I being too familiar?—
I have a fair idea of where you've been:
May to April one unbroken season
of days completely unaccounted for
or frittered away haggling with despair.
But look at us; against all odds, we're here.

Moon Sonnet

Hey, Moon. Remember me? It's been a while
since I last came around for conversation.
My stoop an improvised confessional,
I'd talk and talk and talk and you would listen.
It was thrilling while it lasted. I was young.
Now I've come looking for some help.
The truth is, Moon, a lot's gone wrong;
I was hoping our paths could overlap,
that you might tell me where you find the patience
to get yourself from empty back to full.
(I've watched you, fingernail by fingernail;
eventually you always hit your stride.)
Do you think, if I made a vow of silence,
you'd let me come along once for the ride?

Jenne's Rose

Bizarre garden, bizarre and troubled garden,
see what you can learn from Jenne's rose,
exposing its whole heart as if impervious
to this brief life's collective burden,
deflecting what it can with a perfume
that broadcasts unequivocally *Rose*.
Take it or leave it. It's what I am.
Do you think that strategy could work for us?
Or would we have to back it up with beauty?
But what am I saying? You're a garden.
We're not alike at all. You just need rain
or a sprinkler system, some decent loam.
For you a little light is possibility.
So why these doldrums? You're a garden. Bloom.

Paestum Thunderstorm, Twenty Years On

It was otherworldly. You'd have been rapturous:
lightning over the temples \ wine-dark sky—
no one in that drenched expanse but us

unless you call the thunder a god's voice.
We were soaked completely through, the girls and I.
Even without the storm, you'd have been rapturous,

showing your girls your most beloved place
(that's how I billed it; it's why they came with me)
from our honeymoon travels. No one but us.

But you'd hate the new confinement to the grass.
Back then, we wandered each antiquity;
there's a whole roll of photographs: me, rapturous,

posed at column after column, my face
a likeness of its likeness in your eye.
Of course, it wasn't really only us.

Our girls—you should see them; they're rapturous—
were there as pure desire, standing by,
just as you, pre-disaster, pre-psychosis,
came briefly back in those drenched ruins to us.

Cherries

There's mercy in the decades as they pass,
reducing years of ache to a single afternoon
beneath a cherry tree in a terraced garden:
the cherries seem to ripen while we gaze,
darkening as sunlight starts to fade.
You're talking; I'm waiting for you to realize
what you won't admit for another decade:
love is not a word I wouldn't use
you'll say once I've had daughters, you, a son.
Now there's another decade gone
and I have yet to hear of love
without some qualifier, some double negative.
Perhaps I've stifled it? It's getting late;
no sign of ripeness, just failing light.

Self-Portrait with Lilacs

For me, the lilacs' outburst—once it's here—
always multiplies itself by four,
the faithful scent and starriness and color
a self-perpetuating souvenir

of my spring as a self-styled gypsy/pilgrim
when my wanderings quadrupled their perfume.
I cheered on their mad dash from bud to bloom

in Florence, London, Philadelphia, Boston,
caught Giotto's campanile, then Big Ben,
the Liberty Bell, the USS *Constitution*,
swooning once the lilacs stooped to open,

their purple scepters angling to confer
knighthood on the kneeling, humid air,
sovereignty suspended in each flower

until it seemed to rust and shriveled up.
That year, spring came early to Europe
but in North America, an arctic cold snap
brought spring's arrival to a total stop

with bout after bout of April snow,
the hemispheres in league to let me know
that earth could be counted on to show

somewhere on itself an ardent face,
those lilacs just another gung-ho voice
in 1983's collective chorus
of scope and possibility and purpose.

Not an unmitigated lie
(the earth *was* rife with possibility,
favors seemed to fling themselves at me)

but it did leave quite a few things out
and all that promise made me profligate
with chance after chance. A bit too late
I realized I'd let go of the habit

of giddy and productive expectation.
Who says experience is education?
It doesn't so much teach as wear you down

though it does train you to sniff out solace
in even the most unpropitious place,
to satisfy yourself with less and less.
I'm working on it; the snow's my witness.

The snow's, in fact, my constant intimate
since here it's almost always within sight.
The mountains look ill at ease without it

and even in the valley, we get snowfall
routinely from October straight through April,
our golden leaves and tulips philosophical
about becoming suddenly invisible

precisely when their beauty's at its peak.
Once the snow melts, they bounce right back.
There's no such resilience in a lilac;

at the first touch of snow, its blossoms die.
I've seen it; sometimes we get snow in May.
I consider it a payment of indemnity
for my lilac binge in 1983;

earth has a way of getting even.
You'd think by now the debt would be forgiven
and yet my lilac's still budding in vain.

This year, it's three weeks ahead of schedule
and since there's always snow here in late April
it's pretty much guaranteed to fail.
So I'm both giddy and inconsolable

when the first blossom offers its first star.
I have to press my face to it, since here
the scent's kept secret by the arid air . . .

but soon enough, the sky turns leaden;
white's the world's brief master. Then it's gone
and afterward, I don't know which to mourn:
this spring's lilacs or the deft oblivion

that briefly fended off the world I know.
But it's hard to stay loyal to the snow,
when you see each lilac's bent-over torso,

its unbloomed flowers nearly at the ground
in the posture of an overburdened field hand
or, perhaps, more like a sinner who's atoned.
My lilacs stay like this for days on end.

In truth, I'm amazed that they're still here;
They've never hung on after snow before.
Maybe plants are tempered by the local air

to tolerate the cold after a while . . .
Fiesole's olive trees, for example,
undamaged in the '85 snowfall,
since it always snows a little on their hill.

My lilacs may have settled in at last
or maybe it's timing: snow that melted fast;
early buds that hadn't bloomed in earnest. . . .

Whatever the reason, they're making progress:
the stunted blossoms sag a little less,
look less bedraggled, if not quite gorgeous,
have managed to possess a sort of grace

for all the world like that of lilacs in bloom.
No one passing would suspect a snowstorm
or even that they've suffered any harm.

I wonder if the same is true of me.
Who knows what a passerby would see
if he paid attention? Maybe I
need to take to heart this dark-horse victory,

the lilacs' frank, if muted, splendor.
Surely it's not nothing to endure.
And I get to multiply by four.

II

Orders of Infinity

I remember, as a child, feeling comforted
when my father offered up the word *infinity,*
gratified that something wasn't thwarted
in its efforts to go on and on forever.

I could never bear for things to end
and here was this unprecedented godsend,
suggesting I might sometimes get my way.
Something that goes on and on forever

I took my father's definition literally,
imagining infinity as solid
matter I might actually see
and though I was in those days a believer,

didn't think to link the word to God,
also rumored to go on forever,
but only in the unforthcoming, vague,
shifting syllables sung out in synagogue

where words were rarely sabotaged by meaning
(the true resilience of a holy tongue).
Infinity was English, of *this* world,
not the other one, that's why it thrilled

me. It was not an abstract thing
and this has more or less remained my thinking
which is why, I suppose, I would not take in
my friend, a mathematician's explanation

that infinity actually comes in many sizes.
Think, he tried to tell me, *of equivalencies,*
of points on a line, match "a" to "a,"
"b" to "b," "c" to "c," and so on. . . .

Just because the two might go on endlessly
does not make their essential values the same.
Doesn't it? On what continuum?
Who knew math was such a greedy discipline:

two parts bully, one part sleight-of-hand?
Since when does sense give up without a fight?
What exceeds something without end?
Why expand—and therefore stunt—the infinite?

But it turns out he was right and I was wrong,
though I was never fooled by points on lines;
I learned the lesson in a forest clearing
where an unexpected overflow of stones

deferred to an impassive, cloudless sky.
I'd meant to wander the entire circuit,
but as I approached, the stones would multiply,
every route I staked out incomplete,

until I realized that to reach them all
would have taken an immense amount of time.
Not that I'd have minded; it was beautiful,
the windless air extravagantly calm . . .

the forest one unbroken spell of green
and I was in that whole vast space alone.
But I worried that my traveling companion
(we'd foolishly shown up there at high noon;

she'd gone back to the woods to find some shade)
had long been waiting, wanting to leave;
otherwise, I might have stayed and stayed
at least until I managed to believe

that the place where I was walking was Treblinka.
Should I have warned you? That's where I was;
perhaps I've been a little disingenuous
but it's not a simple thing to write that name.

I wanted to reclaim that perfect calm
and once the name is uttered, calm is lost.
Besides, it *was* a clearing in the forest.
Treblinka

where eight hundred thousand people (mostly mine)
were murdered—seventeen thousand in one day—
was not in evidence. How could it be?
Instead, there is an endless stretch of stone

which you half-believe has always been there
until you read, on some, the names of towns
from which the transports had their origins—
a few (Paris? Turin?) shockingly familiar

but most with names you couldn't say you know.
I kept on the lookout for Salonika,
remembering, from the movie *Shoah,*
a Czech survivor of the Sonderkommando

describing his relief at the arrival
of the Salonika transport, the crackers and jam
he devoured after he was forced to shovel
their owners' bodies into the crematorium. . . .

I'd retained a bungled mental picture:
that quiet man, no younger, dressed the same,
rifling through satchels in a cattle car,
gulping down entire jars of jam. . . .

Inaccurate though it is, it's what remains
the entire sum of all my knowledge
though I did make it to the very edge
of at least one stretch of all those stones.

There's nothing else. The Germans leveled the evidence,
pulled out the train tracks, the barbed-wire fence
entwined with branches of the surrounding forest
(they'd thought they had to hide these camps at first),

dug up the mass graves, burned the bodies
from before they'd built the first crematorium,
plowed the ashes under, built a farm,
even replaced stands and stands of trees,

which were, presumably, cut down again
to make way for whatever it was I saw.
I never did believe it was Treblinka,
had given up, when someone called out in German,

which changed to English when I didn't answer:
"Please, can you tell me where we are?"
he meant—he was standing at the diagram—
where, in relation to each labeled item

and I was helpful. I'd been shown before:
Where we're standing was the railway platform—
those were the tracks; the trains came here—
out there were the gas chambers, the crematorium

I smiled at his wife, daughter, and son,
pointing to the flag on his daughter's T-shirt
that's my country; I'm so glad you like it
suddenly aware of a fresh, acute

disequilibrium inside the atmosphere,
as if the absent wind had changed direction
and blown my flimsy sentences apart.
No, I couldn't tell them where we were.

I left and on the wooded path, broke down—
not—don't mistake me—for the dead—
who will cry for them?—but out of gratitude:
my heart was not unmitigated stone.

Though stoniness might serve as deference
to all the stilled emotion in that place,
a twisted empathy, to be sensationless,
stinting as the stones' arrested eloquence

in their bid to amplify unuttered speech.
Some things are simply out of reach.
And so—what could I do?—I headed out
along the shaded pathway to the parking lot,

already thinking I should turn around,
since I could not have said what I had seen.
For example, had I ever actually found
the name Salonika? Some pale gray stone—

I saw it in my mind, can see it now—
SALONIKA all in caps. I still don't know.
And why were there so many empty stones?
At least they could have borne the names of towns.

I'm not sure how long it finally took
to realize they'd of course run out of names;
there must have been a stone for every person.
Think of the city of Warsaw alone:

something like three hundred thousand victims.
Another eighty thousand from Bialystok.
How could they possibly have names of towns
on each of eight hundred thousand stones?

Later, reading the guidebook in the car,
I learned I'd been way off about that number:
not eight hundred, but seventeen, thousand
stones—the number killed on the worst day.

Seventeen thousand. Eight hundred thousand.
Indistinguishable, at least to me
though they differ by a multiple of forty.
That's when I *got* my friend's infinity,

since both the numbers go on forever
in the shadow world of inverse possibility,
one a smaller, one a greater infinity
of what a cheated earth can never recover.

My friend was entirely right; I was wrong;
try coupling "a" to "a," "b" to "b,"
first among the ashes in that clearing;
next other such clearings, not far away;

then all similar spots, further afield.
Throw in the few who managed to survive
and then—after all, this was the modern world;
they might have paired with anyone alive;

why limit ourselves to European Jews?—
think five, then fifty, generations later:
one infinity a smaller, one a greater
modicum of what we've had to lose.

Think undreamed daydreams, mute conversations,
ungratified indulgences, failed hints,
unwasted afternoons, unwept decisions,
listless doorbells, pots, pens, instruments,

unborrowed finery, unbidden favors,
arcana of the darker arts untaught,
trysts of uninitiated lovers.
Think of anything. It's infinite,

each to its own infinite degree,
this more modest, this more extravagant
in its flagrant incapacity to be.
Why should mathematics be more benevolent

than any other known human pursuit?
There's just so much a number can accrue
before the negative's ambitious undertow
drags it downward to its opposite,

then lower still, with nothing to break its fall,
each unrepeatable descending spiral
an unclaimed outpost of the infinite.
What could be more definite than granite?

Go ahead. Try to count it. Stone by stone
Seventeen thousand, eight hundred thousand.
As you approach, the numbers—even *one*—
all struggle out of order, pull, expand,

their restless values going on forever
as if to get unfinished business done,
so many urgent details to deliver
from their cramped dominions in oblivion.

Villanelle on the Oldest
Known Piece of Writing

There's a real chance I have it wrong,
the oldest known language written down:
All the songs have already been sung.

It sounds apocryphal, but so enticing:
Akkadian? Sumerian? On stone.
There's a real chance I have it wrong.

Still, it would absolve my noiseless tongue
or at least offer some commiseration
if all the songs have already been sung.

Perhaps it's why so many bells are rung:
every hour on the hour, a carillon
(I suppose there's a chance I have it wrong)

helps the air articulate its longing
(The air *is* longing? I'm not alone?)
for all its songs, already sung.

But why, if I've known this all along,
do I keep waiting here, my heart wide open?
There's a real chance I have it wrong.
All the songs have already been sung.

Whitethorn

As always, when I see it, my first thought:
some kids' discarded tissues, helped by wind,
have scattered in the hedge, caught on thorns, not
look! winter's finally at an end
not *this is what it means to bloom for whitethorn.*
It's my greatest failing. I never learn
or, rather, don't apply the things I know,
which is why I have so little to show
for my quickly coming up on fifty years.
But who wants to know that spring is tatters
of dingy whiteness clinging to a briar?
Can't just one bush blaze with fire—
for a single instant—that does not consume?
Or is this my vision? this stingy bloom?

Western Red Cedar: Missing Psalm

God's voice shatters the cedars;
God shattered the cedars of Lebanon.
  —Psalm 29:6

Who would have the heart to shatter these?
Too bad David couldn't know these cedars
(Jacob's green-winged angels *and* their ladders,
so thick, you can't quite catch them take the skies;
lacework always hides the last few rungs),
nothing like their puny Lebanese cousins.
Who can know what sinuous horizons
they'd have smuggled into David's songs?
He might not have heard God's voice at all
in the sudden, giddy clamor of his own.
That's why God kept these trees confidential.
But now God laments that missing psalm.
Once in a while, He'd like to daydream
about the wondrous things He could have done.

Variations on Variations

(Picasso's Las Meninas, *1957)*

I

It could have been anything: he was tired
of coming up with projects of his own.
Seventy-five years old. Running scared.

Nostalgic for his birthplace all of a sudden.
Afraid he'd die soon. Unprepared.
Maybe he simply wanted in. . . .

It *was* his kind of turf, sublime *and* weird,
left behind in long off-limits Spain
(where the Popular Front had been elected, cheered,

but lacked sufficient ruthlessness to reign).
Nothing ever *was* as it appeared
and he felt obliged to make this point again

and again and again. Or maybe he was just bored
with his blue, blue view (the Mediterranean)
or maybe his trademark doves had disappeared.

II

Or maybe he was saying: this is *mine*
mine and not the bully Falangistas':
mine despite geography (or,
rather, as its birthright) despite
the fledgling Nazis' tryout bombs,
which—though he'd broken his own rule
of being as a painter apolitical
and raced to condemn them in his World's
Fair mural (*Guernica,* of course, 1937)—
continued and continued to rain down

III

Mine—not just by virtue of a childhood
spent scrutinizing its magnificence,
at his father, the art professor's, side—
but *mine* by dint of potent revelation:
the chameleon instinct of the infanta's
skin—how it routinely gallivants
behind closed doors among extremes
of blue and gray and green, usurping
a yellow from a fogged-in sun
in order to assuage a saffron gown

IV

Mine, the serving woman's two-eyed profile,
mine her extra nostril, extra limb,
mine the extravagant and shrill supply
of a prized variety of African textile
the infanta's mother—unhinged by pregnancy—
had commissioned nightly in her lurid dreams

V

Mine the vast and boldly colored distance
from the far too temperate original,
condemned to servitude in gray and ocher
in a country its own painter wouldn't recognize

VI

Mine—court painter though Velázquez was;
besides, if you look closely at his all-encompassing
deceptively entitled *Las Meninas*
(*Maids of Honor?* what maids of honor?)
you'll see the king and queen—if they appear at all—
as afterthoughts reflected in a mirror

overshadowed by a mystery figure—
cape suavely draping off his shoulder—
scoping the layout from his center door.

(Actually, they're reflections of reflections;
there has to be another larger mirror,
invisible, except in its command
of the entire vista, which means that
everything we're seeing is inverted. . . .
But isn't the mirror where *we* stand?
It must be, since we can see the painter
in the foreground, at his easel, palette in hand.)

VII

Maybe the natty figure is Picasso:
Velázquez always knew he was coming,
hence the convenient, open door

VIII

or maybe the canvas just needed a cleaning;
and—at such a distance—those ebullient colors
were the closest Picasso could get to restoration . . .
in which case, it wasn't colossal hubris,
but a sudden impulse toward preservation
that made him think Spain's
quintessential masterpiece
required a little touch-up at his hand.

IX

Besides, you could also call it humble:
definitive proof for all posterity
(mathematics leaves no room for flattery):
one Velázquez = infinite Picassos
or how many is it? forty? fifty?

a whole section of the Barcelona museum,
fifty-eight (I looked it up)

X

or maybe Picasso *is* showing off—
the extraordinarily wide-ranging ambit
of his tour-de-force imagination:
a never-ending entourage of canvases
leaping from Velázquez' measly one . . .

XI

or maybe it was just a lucky break,
Picasso taking advantage of the situation:
you see a door ajar, you wander in. . . .

XII

Or maybe, by his time, the unseen mirror
was full of hairline cracks and imperfections;
Picasso just recorded what he saw:
the accidental prisms splitting colors,
distorting images, blunting details. . . .

XIII

So much can happen in three hundred years
usually so little of it good . . .

though sometimes happy changes can surprise;
for example, poor Picasso died
with his *Meninas* still in exile
(he wouldn't have his work in Fascist Spain),

Guernica a refugee at MOMA . . .
teaching New York's aesthetes (me

among them, my actual garret
within walking distance in one of midtown's
hold-out tenements, long since replaced
by steel and glass) that outrage
can produce great art. . . .

And just the other day, in the Republic of Spain
(the very title would have thrilled Picasso)
not only were there national elections
but no right-wing generals staged a coup
when socialists—the incumbents! imagine!—won

XIV

and smack in the center of Barcelona
the Museu Picasso holds its ground:
its pièce de résistance: the freed *Meninas*.

XV

A tribute?
A victory?
An inside joke?
A public
self-flagellation?

XVI

Forgive me, Pablo
—may I call you Pablo?
I'm thinking if you
can turn a princess
green, I can address
you by your name—
anyway, forgive me
that despite the fact
that—working graveyard

in 1983, armed with a
not-quite-kosher student
membership (fifteen
dollars for the entire year!)—
I saw *Les Demoiselles
d'Avignon* on average
four times a week
(usually in the break between
free movies) along with
the green-striped *Girl
before a Mirror* (maybe
she too comes from
Velázquez? She's significantly
darker in reflection)

not to mention growing
up in Philadelphia, bewildered
by your outsized musicians
Is that a piano? I think it's a piano

I love more than any of your exploits
those radical revivals of *Meninas*—
which I've seen on precisely two occasions
at an interval of twenty-three years—
and I barely remember the first sighting.

XVII

Maybe it requires half a lifetime
to be susceptible to the oblique appeal
of the ancillary, the subordinate,
the parenthetical, the deviation,
the anxious bluster of communication
with what by definition can't be reached

XVIII

but what can I tell you, at forty-six
(five years I've been meaning to write this poem)
I walked into the first room of *Meninas*
and would have had to lean against a wall
or even turn away to compose myself
had my eight-year-old not pulled me out of it,
shouting gleefully (she'd been so dutiful
at the Prado) *Mommy we know this painting.*

Maybe it *was* the half hour or so
we'd spent just days before with the Velázquez
that left me so off-balance, so defenseless
against the paintings' staggering bravado,
I devoured those *Meninas* like a gossip-starved
interloper in a swanky inner circle,

pressing each canvas for its promised trove
of juicy, scandal-mongering detail
from that first indiscretion in black and white
through the tantrums of its prima-donna offspring,
vying for top billing, for the most outlandish colors
as they zigzagged in a whirlwind down the wall

XIX

because I like knowing that a masterpiece
is an ongoing and fluid thing

that we're not stuck
in our imploding moment

that a seemingly expired binge of rapture
can set a train of gorgeousness in motion

resurrect our sidelined calls to action.
Let the foolhardy cry *derivative*

I say it proves we're not alone,
that, if there's a God, He has a generous streak;

He's always willing to share the inexhaustible . . .
to look on as monumental outbursts

even some from the most humble origins
argue forever, converse forever

XX

that an unapologetic imagination
with a modicum of stamina will thrive
and a person with the slightest bit of nerve
can engage it—look at me!—in conversation. . . .
I—even I—get to write *mine*
when I mean *yours,* to stop floundering
and lose myself in your daredevil line
as if I too were in on its enduring
antidote to rampant shabbiness.
I'm begging, Pablo. Sneak me inside. . . .
I won't ask what you asked of Velázquez.
Just make me a handmaid. I'm not proud.
See? I'm tidying up, scrounging dessert;
now let me eavesdrop and think it's art.

Flanders Sonnet

Some say these masters—labeled primitives
by the unsubtle show-offs who succeeded them—
used magnifying glasses to achieve these thumb-
nail castles, bridges, barges, perfect archives
of fifteenth-century Flanders so minute
the eye can barely see them without aid.
How else produce each swath of gold brocade,
each glint of light deflected off a facet
of ruby in the gold-filigree diadem
held over Mary by a diligent angel?
Still, how easily this fretwork Bethlehem
repeats her crown around her baby's head,
as if halo and stone were interchangeable,
the earth ethereal, the sacred solid.

In a Storm, Revisiting Isaiah

Though your sins be as scarlet,
they shall be as white as snow.
    —Isaiah 1:18

by which he meant—though how he could have known
in that unprepossessing climate
is a mystery—the kind of absolution
granted by a snowstorm at its height:
the earth relieved of all it knows or wonders,
each item in its arsenal displaced,
the vote unanimous (no dissenters)
to yield, as white's unstinting ultimatum
muffles every flaw, dissolves the past;
rooftop, lamppost, fence—nothing endures
against its all-encompassing delirium,
scarlet not just hidden but impossible
until the snow melts and it's all visible
as, one by one, we reclaim our scars.

Todas las Puertas

Even then, I knew it was ridiculous,
after all that traveling, to drag
my eight-year-old daughter on another bus

to see what you can see on synagogue
doorways anywhere: *this is the gate*
to God (it's mentioned in a makeshift catalog

of Jewish sites in Spain, a xeroxed pamphlet
I leafed through in a bookshop in Toledo)
the righteous will enter through it,

still clearly legible in Hebrew
from above the doorway of a house of prayer:
the one proof of our sojourn in Trujillo,

now on the pharmacy in the main square
(a beautiful square, as it turns out, medieval,
the walkways porticoed, the church austere).

We circled many times but found no lintel
inscribed with anything that looked like Hebrew
and finally gave up, climbed the hill,

the steepest belltower, took in the view:
high desert interrupted by pink stone,
once lorded over by a Moorish parvenu

whose castle outlived Christian dereliction.
Siesta over, we headed back down
hoping the tourist office would reopen,

rechecking doorways as we stood in line
in case we'd overlooked our stone before.
To our surprise, the helpful woman

knew all about what we were looking for.
It was inside the pharmacy, not outside,
a few hundred meters off the square

on a street we'd somehow managed to avoid.
I'd read too quickly, never planning
to *go* to Trujillo, my Spanish not good,

and clearly gotten all the details wrong.
Meanwhile, this was Saturday afternoon
and the pharmacy was closed till Monday morning,

by which time we'd long have left the region
for Córdoba, where walls of Hebrew, carved
with quintessential Moorish complication,

are on display, amazingly preserved
inside a structure many times remodeled.
(The craftsmen must have thought such art deserved

safekeeping underneath the walls they paneled
into somber piety, befitting prayers
of members of the shoemakers' guild

to Saints Crispin and Crispiano, their protectors.)
It was a priest who finally discovered them
after five hundred or so years—

snippets—still intact—of Hebrew psalm—
as chunks of mortar crumbling off a wall
reopened age-old threats to Christendom

from the unreconstructed infidel.
This time, they received due recognition.
But I, who'd see them, nonetheless would still

lament my one unwitnessed Hebrew stone
on the doorway to the storeroom of a pharmacy
in a tiny Extremadura town.

Not that I gave up easily, I'd gotten my way
by being insistent earlier on;
I had the woman telephone, told her I'd pay

if the pharmacist were willing to reopen.
But he'd already left for the day
and lived quite a distance outside town.

No one else, she told me, had the key
(a statement I wish I'd thought to question,
since, surely, a more local employee

would have had some means of keeping the place open
on days when the owner couldn't get there).
But that day there was nothing to be done,

so we finally gave up, took the walking tour,
which led us through the oldest part of town—
what had been, they told us, the Jewish quarter—

where bulging upper stories seemed to join
across the narrow streets, blocking sunlight
(so overwhelming everywhere else in town)

from streets so crooked, archways so tight,
we had to angle sideways to get through,
keeping, all the while, on the lookout

for even the most questionable clue—
a dent (maybe from a mezuzah?) in a doorpost—
that a single house had once contained a Jew.

Clearly doorposts—even stone ones—don't last,
since a mezuzah had to hang on every one
and I swear I looked at every doorpost

in every *juderia* left in Spain—
all perfectly smooth, no dents, no cuts,
no evidence of what there must have been.

It's a prayer an observant Jew recites
twice daily (*when you lie down and when you rise*):
you shall write them on your doorposts and on your gates.

Even many of us who aren't religious
know the entire paragraph by heart.
Perhaps it was they, themselves, the Jews,

hoping to remain somehow unhurt,
who pulled their own mezuzahs off their doors
after they pretended to convert.

Others managed to get out with the Moors
to confuse unlikely ports with Jewish Spanish:
Rabat, Salonika, Tunis, Algiers.

Even now, peppered with Turkish,
its singsong jangles neighborhoods in Istanbul
and further inland, rough with the harsh

intrusion of a local Slavic guttural,
confuses certain streets in Sarajevo
with words that would be wholly comprehensible

in Salamanca, Segovia, Toledo,
if its speakers were to come back with the keys
that stayed with them in Smyrna, in Aleppo,

Salonika, Dubrovnik for six centuries
to houses temporarily left behind.
I'm told they're heirlooms in certain families,

some stored in precious boxes—velvet-lined—
or kept on hand beside a current door.
Who knows? Maybe one of them would find

its long-lost soul mate still watching over
a heavy wooden portal in Castile,
Andalus, Extremadura, Navarre.

Unlikely, I admit, but not impossible.
Some things in this world stay as they are.
Okay, not many, but at least a handful:

take, for example, the still water
in the pink stone mikvah in Besalú.
You go to the little tourist office there,

say *mikvah,* and they hand the key to you,
walk you to the door and point the way,
and when you reach the pools (there are two,

one to clean you first? and one to purify?)
something that you couldn't otherwise know
takes shape beneath the narrow slip of sky

the window-slit reluctantly lets through:
how an actual bit of time each month was spent
by every Jewish matron in Besalú.

And briefly, what I'd always found abhorrent—
the monthly rite of women's purification—
became a ritual extravagant

with the dreaminess of anticipation—
one's entire body immersed below
water on pink stone in preparation

for the certain pleasure that would follow . . .
it is the voice of my beloved that knocketh . . .
water lapping against limb and torso

myrrh upon the handles of the lock. . . .
More likely, of course, for the haggard women
with their many children, it was simply a break,

unless it was just one more obligation
among endless tasks and errands to fulfill,
and maybe, for those women who were barren,

it was punishing, this monthly ritual,
as they'd hope: *perhaps this time, perhaps now*
while other women dreaded the brutal

overtures this mikvah would allow
and hoped for a sign of impure residue
(perhaps some faked it? I wonder how)

to render them, for one week more, taboo.
Needless to say, no one can know
what any woman felt like in Besalú

more than half a millennium ago,
but in the changeless rigor of that place
those scores of women converge on you

with a rare—if imprecise—assertiveness
requiring very little imagination.
And this, you remember, is the grace

of belonging to a stubborn, hidebound nation,
a provincial grace perhaps, perhaps hard-won
and tainted by tenacious superstition

but still: this sense of something as your own
that's actually existed for millennia
is such an enduring consolation

in the daunting jumble of ephemera
that day-to-day existence has become.
Not that the oddments of diaspora,

an accidental pool or tower or dome,
could ever be said really to matter;
I know this, don't I? My medium

has never, after all, been stone or water.
What a fool to go all the way to Spain,
not to mention dragging my youngest daughter,

to learn what I already should have known
from a museum director, of all people, in Toledo,
after I begged his assistant on the telephone

for a chance to see the Sinagoga del Tránsito
despite the ongoing restoration.
(It was easy to get the number from the two

functionaries at tourist information;
it got rid of me, and would lead nowhere.)
Despite my Spanish, she heard my desperation.

I'm sorry, she said; *they're working on the floor,*
it's simply not possible to go in.
I'd be happy, I said, *to stand in the door-*

way. I'm an American poet, Jewish Spain
was supposed to be something of a muse.
She put me on hold, then came back on.

How soon could I get there? Her boss—
the director—would be glad to receive me.
Next I was shaking a hand: *A las poetas*—

I am *not* making this up; it's how he greeted me—
todas las puertas están abiertas.
Then he proceeded to read Cavafy.

This morning, when you called I was reading this;
beautiful isn't it? But the Spanish was hard
(a glimpse of something? someone? in a looking glass?)

and I was reeling from what I'd heard:
to poets all doors are open; he was right;
later, of course, I realized he'd prepared

the statement as a welcome, a tribute;
he hadn't meant to expose me as a fraud.
But, think about it: why *should* a poet,

whose specialty is infiltration, need
a museum director's dispensation
or a signpost to the gate of God?

And why did I, even after that conversation,
keep traipsing after every scrap or tidbit
of unnecessary outward confirmation?

I know it's the words that are the gate
and not the doorways they've been carved above;
still it's one thing to intimate

and quite another to arrive.
Maybe I've taken for granted for too long
the ease with which the words themselves survive;

surely my postmodern American tongue
is an even less likely repository
for a three-thousand-year-old Hebrew song

than a stone in a medieval Spanish pharmacy?
But what's enough? What's ever enough?
Poetry can hardly guarantee

safe passage when you're herded off a cliff.
Toledo. Roca Tarpeya. No return.
I can't remember now. Were they pushed off,

or did they jump, preferring not to burn?
All I remember clearly is the view:
a stunning sudden drop, the stark ravine

and behind me, exquisite gold Toledo.
Nothing registered. It was serene.
Perhaps that lintel—had I seen it—in Trujillo

would have lodged in my imagination
as a marker for that unacknowledged grave
and all the others scattered across Spain

which no one told me about. Should I even believe
the proprietor of the tiny Jewish gift shop
who seemed to be a sort of one-man archive

of Jewish Toledo? He drew me a map,
though it's not at all hard to find that spot;
there *were* pogroms in Toledo: I looked them up

but I found few details beyond each date
(1212, 1391, 1449)
and words like "mass murder," "bloodbath," "riot,"

nothing about a cliff; as for my stone
there's one exactly like it in San Marco,
a fifteen-minute walk from the pension

where I lived in Florence twenty years ago;
and though I spent hours on that museum's stairs
(I've yet to have my fill of the Fra Angelico

angel catching Mary unawares),
I never bothered with the floor below—
its architectural details, stones and pillars—

and only discovered remnants of the ghetto
on a recent trip, when I took a right
instead of a left and walked straight into Hebrew

on travertine, reading: *this is the gate*—
a dime a dozen in the places where Jews pray.
But I had reasons for wanting to see it

on the wall of a contemporary pharmacy.
Psalms are believed to heal the sick;
the pious recite them every day

to cure the ailing; it's a Yiddish joke:
If psalms could cure, they'd sell in pharmacies.
Yiddish speakers tended toward the caustic

about the efficacy of songs of praise
after centuries of fruitless ministrations
and *they*'re my people, not the worldly rabbis

who were Spain's poets, viziers, mathematicians
with elaborately carved houses of prayer;
my connections were their poorest relations,

whose synagogues, even, were threadbare,
their mikvahs dank and dark, their livings hard,
their only luxury the kind of humor

that could turn an unassuming Yiddish word
into a twisting knife, a wrecking crew, a goad—
my father-in-law, once asked the word for mustard,

responded *Mustard? We didn't have bread!*—
intonation a precision instrument—
That's what you have to see? The gate to God?—

for finely tuned gradations of complaint—
Come with me to the cemetery; I'll show you.
He didn't much go in for sentiment

which was fortunate, since he had no
mementos whatsoever from his youth,
except for memory's quicksilver residue.

His shtetl disappeared with his death,
unless some Polish neighbor is still alive
who remembers when each market stall or booth

was the fiefdom of a yenta who'd survive
on equal shares of inventory and scolding.
There's nothing left at all, not even a grave—

except that *noisy as a Jewish wedding*
is still a Polish way of saying *din*.
The headstones were carted off for building

foundations to extend the railway line
that would carry those market women away,
along with their husbands—loath to abandon

the holy texts they studied night and day—
their unkempt, incorrigible children,
butcher, tailor, factory owner, rabbi,

but why enumerate them? Everyone—
including my father-in-law's father, brother,
stepmother, half-sisters—the whole town

was taken on one transport or another.
The way my father-in-law always told it,
he himself, wanting to help his father,

or, at the very least, find out his fate
deliberately got himself onto a train
that ended up at Auschwitz. He found out.

And what I now know, having been to Spain,
is that in another half millennium
if someone comes looking for a stone

in Poland, carved, say, with a bit of psalm—
someone who thinks words can open doors—
he or she will find bucolic charm

(assuming there are still forests and pastures,
assuming our ill-treated earth endures)
but be completely shielded from the horrors

that for an impossible span of years
were in those forests and pastures commonplace,
though she'll have read books, seen films, heard lectures

about the makeshift factories that could "process"
thousands of people in a day.
But who am I kidding? It's ridiculous

to place this half a millennium away
when—what is it now—sixty-four, sixty-three?
(was it December '42 or '43?)

years since my father-in-law went after his family
(they were already dead, needless to say)
and while his stories have stayed with me,

left bits of me permanently at bay,
how much could I really say I know?
I'm a Jew, after all; for me history

is personal, a living business, *now*
is always partly in the thrall of *then*.
I myself escaped the bonds of Pharaoh,

crossed the Red Sea, stood near the mountain
to hear the Ten Commandments in God's voice—
or so insists my grandiose tradition

so bossily I half-remember the noise.
I've been known to say *it must have been on Sinai*
when I can't place a familiar Jewish face

(though Jewish summer camp is a lot more likely;
or long-forgotten youth group conventions)
but if I was on Sinai, then where was I

when we were crowded on those cliffs, those trains
and where, precisely, am I now?
I certainly can't face the botched dimensions

of the current—also drastic—status quo—
and this time, we aren't without blame. . . .
Clearly in the face of real fiasco

one needs something more potent than a poem;
my ancestors were right: *if psalms could cure*. . . .
And yet there's bounty in the strict regime—

three times daily—of ancient prayer;
however much it hovers toward the rote,
it's building up the stamina to conjure

the steady prospect of a tête-à-tête
with a rapt, if not entirely obliging, listener
just beyond the outline of a gate. . . .

Surely, even a long shot is a cure
for something? Not mere anodyne, but thrill.
Poetic transport. What might open a door

albeit inconclusive or ephemeral
to an otherwise undocumented heart.
Witnesses say those transports were full

of serious praying, at least at their start,
the two kinds of transport intimate
though one would think they'd keep as far apart

as geometric planes that never meet.
Joined parallel lines. What I need here:
Todas las puertas. Every gate.

Perhaps they're underneath a wall somewhere—
some house of prayer in Isfahan, Baku—
just about to show through cracking plaster;

or maybe they're even in plain view
in an abandoned shul that has no minyan,
like the *Licho Dodi* painted around each window

of the synagogue I stood in in Tykocin,
whose words I tried and failed to read aloud.
I'd wanted to fulfill our long tradition

of honoring the dead by praising God
and magnifying His name in their name.
But though, the day before that, I'd stood dry-eyed,

reading hand-made plaques with perfect calm
in the forest where the people of that town
had been shot and buried by a thorough team

of the famously efficient Einsatzgruppen,
in the synagogue I couldn't get beyond
the first few phrases of the prayer's first line—

a prayer I knew by heart—beginning to end—
had sung for a good four decades at least.
It was as if the words refused to sound;

perhaps they thought the people in that forest—
even if they had to go unnamed—
had a right to someone who could pray in earnest,

as did the walls themselves, once accustomed—
three times a day—to honest prayer.
Still, if walls have memories, they've dimmed.

But I felt lucky just to find them there,
lines of Hebrew painted on them all,
each mute letter a potential door

to something otherwise impalpable
that shuts, as I approach it, in my face.
But maybe one of them will have a peephole,

some opening, some tiny circle of glass.
If I'm quick enough (I'm not) I'll get a peek.
Even then—I'd probably just see chaos.

Maybe the definition of the tzaddik
(one who'll enter the gate, one of the righteous)
is someone with the wherewithal to look

beyond the disappointing obvious—
or maybe he also sees just what we see
but manages to bless it nonetheless:

we do have a blessing for any contingency—
my favorite's the one for a shooting star—
belief's not everything, it's worth a try . . .

of course, first you have to *see* the star,
but there's also one for lightning or a rainbow,
encountering a brilliant Torah scholar,

hearing news of a death, dodging a blow.
Maybe there's an esoteric prayer
that restores what you've forgotten that you know

in your admittedly justifiable despair.
Maybe an actual tzaddik, incognito,
is right now reciting it somewhere—

over and over, the entire way through,
and won't stop until you can decipher
the precise coordinates from which to view

your own undisputed, if modest, share
of a wholly uncorrupted place to go
from a vantage point so intimate and clear

you'll know which shrubs and herbs and grasses grow
in each forest, cliff, ravine, and pasture,
how, at any given instant, one or two

from which you could extract a foolproof cure
for any trouble you might undergo
would just be coming into fullest flower.

Meanwhile tiny flakes that look like snow
have begun collecting in your tzaddik's hair.
If he notices, it doesn't show.

He's so deeply focused on his prayer,
he won't see the message breaking through
the walls' and ceiling's decomposing plaster

which means you have no choice; it's up to you.
What can you do? You stare and stare.
Maybe you'll see a hand-carved line of Hebrew

unread for a millennium or more,
dazzling as the pools at Besalú
with the same compulsion to make you pure

and just below it: an insistent arrow
to a flimsy, but pristine, still open door
or maybe there's nothing urgent, nothing new;

indeed, it's almost boringly familiar:
the gate to God the righteous enter through;
luckily your tzaddik is still at his prayer:

tzitzis flying, shuckling to and fro,
he won't stop even for a breath of air
just continue and continue and continue